HANDS—ON JOBS

FARMERS

JOYCE JEFFRIES

PowerKiDS press.

New York

Published in 2016 by The Rosen Publishing Group, Inc.
29 East 21st Street, New York, NY 10010

First Edition

Editor: Katie Kawa
Book Design: Reann Nye

Photo Credits: Cover, pp. 3–24 (background texture) Toluk/Shutterstock.com; cover Michael DeYoung/Blend Images/Getty Images; p. 5 Zorandim/ Shutterstock.com; p. 7 (top) stavros images/Shutterstock.com; p. 7 (middle) lcswart/ Shutterstock.com; p. 7 (bottom) Taina Sohlman/Shutterstock.com; p. 9 Air Images/ Shutterstock.com; p. 11 (poultry farm) Naffarts/Shutterstock.com; p. 11 (fish farm) Vladislav Gajic/Shutterstock.com; p. 11 (crop farm) Sea Wave/Shutterstock.com; p. 13 (main) Ratikova/Shutterstock.com; p. 13 (inset) Fotokostic/Shutterstock.com; p. 14 bibiphoto/Shutterstock.com; p. 15 Jan Scherders/Blend Images/Getty Images; p. 17 (farmer) Tom Wang/Shutterstock.com; p. 17 (background) Pinkyone/ Shutterstock.com; p. 18 Hassel Sinar/Shutterstock.com; p. 19 Hill Street Studios/ Blend Images/Getty Images; p. 21 John Fedele/Blend Images/Getty Images; p. 22 Monty Rakusen/Cultura/Getty Images.

Library of Congress Cataloging-in-Publication Data

Cataloging-in-Publication Data

Jeffries, Joyce.
Farmers / by Joyce Jeffries.
p. cm. — (Hands-on jobs)
Includes index.
ISBN 978-1-5081-4359-8 (pbk.)
ISBN 978-1-5081-4360-4 (6-pack)
ISBN 978-1-5081-4361-1 (library binding)
1. Farmers — Juvenile literature. 2. Agriculture — Juvenile literature. I. Jeffries, Joyce. II. Title.
S519.J44 2016
630'.2'03—d23

Manufactured in the United States of America

CPSIA Compliance Information: Batch #BW16PK: For Further Information contact Rosen Publishing, New York, New York at 1-800-237-9932

CONTENTS

A FARMER'S LIFE

Working on a farm isn't easy. Farmers often work from sunrise to sunset when it's time to plant and **harvest** crops. Farmers who work with livestock have to take care of the animals every day. Farmers also use many machines, and it's often their job to keep the machines running properly.

Working on a farm means spending a lot of time outside and doing a lot of work with your hands. If you like gardening or taking care of animals, you might make a good farmer. Some kids grow up on farms, so they learn to be farmers at a young age.

DIGGING DEEPER

There are around 2 million farms in the United States today.

A career as a farmer is sometimes dirty and **dangerous**, but it can be fun and rewarding, too.

THE FIRST FARMERS

Farmers have been around for thousands of years. In fact, farming, which is also known as agriculture, was one of the most important **developments** in human history. As farmers began to grow crops and raise livestock, people no longer had to follow and hunt wild animals or gather wild plants. This allowed them to settle in one place, creating the first towns and cities.

Farming continues to be one of the most important jobs in the world today. Farmers grow the crops and raise the animals people around the world use for food. They also grow crops, such as cotton, used for fiber to make cloth.

DIGGING DEEPER

Historians believe people first began to farm at the end of the last ice age, which was over 11,000 years ago.

Farming is one of the world's oldest and most important jobs.

FARM FAMILIES

Farming is often a family business. Around 90 **percent** of farms in the United States are run by individuals or families instead of companies. People who live on farms make up about 2 percent of the U.S. population.

Because farming is often a career passed down within families, many young people are raised to be farmers. In 2013, a **survey** of America's young farmers showed 94 percent of them believed they'd be farmers for life. That same survey showed 90 percent of young farmers want their children to be farmers someday, too. Some families have owned farms in the United States for hundreds of years!

DIGGING DEEPER

Over 66 percent of people who work on farms in the United States live on farms, too. The rest are hired farmworkers.

Growing up on a farm teaches young people most of the skills they need to be successful farmers when they get older.

DIFFERENT FARMS, DIFFERENT FARMERS

Not all farmers do the same kind of work. This is because not all farms are the same. There are many different kinds of farms in just the United States alone.

Some farmers grow only crops, such as fruits and vegetables. Others combine growing crops with raising livestock. There are many specialized livestock farmers. These include dairy farmers and poultry, or chicken, farmers. Another kind of farmer raises fish for food. This kind of farming is called aquaculture. Some kinds of farms go by other names, such as an orchard, which is where fruit is grown on trees. People who work at an orchard are farmers, too.

DIGGING DEEPER

A ranch is a large farm where cows, sheep, or horses are raised.

poultry farm

crop farm

Although these places look very different, they're all farms.

fish farm

A GROSS WAY TO GROW CROPS

Crop farming is one of the most important kinds of farming. Farmers who grow crops have to learn what kinds of crops grow well in the soil where they live. They also have to make sure those crops get enough water and **nutrients** to grow from tiny seeds into the food we eat.

Farmers use fertilizer, which is something added to the soil to help plants grow. Some fertilizers are synthetic, or man-made. However, one kind of fertilizer comes from animals. It's called manure, and it's the waste that comes out of an animal's body. Crop farmers who also raise animals have a lot of manure to fertilize their plants!

DIGGING DEEPER

Only a certain amount of manure is good for the soil. Manure contains harmful **chemicals** that can make water and air toxic, or deadly. There are rules for how much manure farmers can have on their land at one time.

synthetic fertilizer

Manure helps crops grow, but it's also very messy and can be harmful. Farmers need to wear gloves around manure to stay safe.

WHAT DO DAIRY FARMERS DO?

Farmers often get manure for their crops from the cows that live on their farm. Cows are an important part of farms around the United States.

On dairy farms, cows are raised for their milk. Years ago, farmers milked cows by hand. Now, most dairy farms use machines to milk cows. However, farmers still have plenty of work to do on dairy farms. They feed the cows and take care of baby cows, or calves. They also clean the stalls where the cows live and collect manure from the cows.

DIGGING DEEPER

Cows on most U.S. dairy farms are milked two to three times each day.

Dairy farmers take good care of their cows so the cows stay healthy and produce good milk.

15

SCIENCE ON THE FARM

Milking machines on dairy farms are just one piece of technology that's made life easier for farmers. Farmers use tractors and trucks to move equipment, or tools, around their land. Tractors can carry plows for breaking up dirt or manure spreaders for safely handling manure. Farmers also use a tool called a grain combine. This machine separates the **kernel** of a grain from the straw.

Science has also played a big part in helping farmers. **Genetic engineering**, such as **crossbreeding**, is used on many farms throughout the United States. It helps farmers produce crops that are healthier than they once were.

DIGGING DEEPER

Modern farmers use computers to control the machines that feed cows. The computers make sure the cows get the right amount of food each day.

IRRIGATION

Pipes carry water to dry areas of land.

———

Sprinklers water the dry land.

GENETIC ENGINEERING

Crossbreeding creates crops that produce more food.

———

New plants are created that are less likely to die from diseases, or sicknesses.

MODERN AMERICAN FARMING

INTEGRATED PEST MANAGEMENT

Pests, such as certain bugs, are killed using natural predators (spiders, ladybugs) to avoid using harmful chemicals.

COMPUTER TECHNOLOGY

Computers control farm equipment.

———

Programs match crops and soil types to get the most out of the least amount of land.

These are just some of the ways farmers use science and technology to make their farms more productive.

SAFETY ON THE FARM

Farmers need to know how to safely operate the machines they use. Otherwise, they could get hurt. One of the most important safety rules on a farm is to turn off all machines before touching their working parts.

Farmers spend most of their time outside. They have to deal with harsh weather and high heat. They often have to lift heavy things. Working on a farm isn't for everyone. However, if you like doing work outside, it might be the right job for you. If you enjoy caring for animals, farming might also be a good career choice.

DIGGING DEEPER

Farmers often wear gloves and goggles for safety while they're working.

Farmers know to be calm and move slowly around livestock. Knowing how to care for animals is an important skill all livestock farmers need to have.

SCHOOLS FOR FARMERS

Although most farmers learn how to do their job by working on farms while growing up, many of them still go to college. Agricultural colleges throughout the United States teach young men and women the tools they need to become good farmers.

Students at an agricultural college learn about plant diseases, different kinds of crops, and how to care for livestock. They can also learn about genetic engineering, the business side of farming, and other important topics. If you want to become a farmer, an agricultural college is a great place to start.

DIGGING DEEPER

Government programs have been created in the United States to train new farmers by pairing them with people who've been farming for a long time.

Years ago, most farmers didn't go to college. Now, going to college is often an important step on the way to becoming a successful farmer.

FUN WITH FARMING

Does being a farmer sound like fun? There are many things you can do now to prepare for a career on a farm. You can try growing plants in your backyard or in a community garden. If you have a pet, you can take care of it like a farmer cares for their animals.

If you live near a farm, you can visit with an adult to see what it's like. If farming seems like the right job for you, keep learning as much as you can about the skills you'll need to succeed in this career.

GLOSSARY

chemical: Matter that can be mixed with other matter to cause changes.

crossbreeding: Mixing two kinds of plants to form a new one.

dangerous: Not safe.

development: The act or process of growing or causing something to grow.

genetic engineering: The science of making changes to the basic building blocks of a living thing to produce a desired result.

harvest: To gather crops after they've grown.

kernel: A whole grain or seed of a cereal, such as wheat or corn.

nutrient: Something taken in by a plant or animal that helps it grow and stay healthy.

percent: A part of a whole. One percent is one part in a hundred.

survey: An activity in which many people are asked questions in order to gather facts about what most people think about something.

INDEX

WEBSITES

Due to the changing nature of Internet links, PowerKids Press has developed an online list of websites related to the subject of this book. This site is updated regularly. Please use this link to access the list: www.powerkidslinks.com/hoj/farm